To:

_____

From:

_____

Date:

_____

MW01130116

GOD CARES
When I'm Afraid

Stormie Omartian
Bestselling Author of *What Happens When I Talk to God?*

Artwork by Shari Warren

HARVEST HOUSE PUBLISHERS
EUGENE, OREGON

God Cares When I'm Afraid

Text copyright © 2019 by Stormie Omartian
Artwork copyright © 2019 by Shari Warren

HARVEST KIDS is a registered trademark of The Hawkins Children's LLC. Harvest House Publishers, Inc., is the exclusive licensee of the federally registered trademark HARVEST KIDS.

Published by Harvest House Publishers
Eugene, Oregon 97408
www.harvesthousepublishers.com

Back cover author photo © Michael Gomez Photography
Cover design by Left Coast Design
Interior design by Chad Dougherty

The Scripture verse on page 3 is taken from the New King James Version®. Copyright © 1982 by Thomas Nelson, Inc. Used by permission. All rights reserved.

ISBN 978-0-7369-7640-4 (hardcover)

Library of Congress Cataloging-in-Publication Data

Names: Omartian, Stormie, author.
Title: God cares when I'm afraid / Stormie Omartian ; artwork by Shari Warren.
Description: Eugene : Harvest House Publishers, 2019.
Identifiers: LCCN 2019016408 (print) | LCCN 2019019877 (ebook) | ISBN 9780736976411 (ebook) | ISBN 9780736976404 (hardcover)
Subjects: LCSH: Children—Religious life—Juvenile literature. | Fear—Religious aspects—Christianity—Juvenile literature. | Fear in children—Juvenile literature.
Classification: LCC BV4571.3 (ebook) | LCC BV4571.3 .O425 2019 (print) | DDC 242/.62—dc23
LC record available at https://lccn.loc.gov/2019016408.

All rights reserved. No part of this publication may be reproduced, stored in a retrieval system, or transmitted in any form or by any means—electronic, mechanical, digital, photocopy, recording, or any other—except for brief quotations in printed reviews, without the prior permission of the publisher.

Printed in China

19 20 21 22 23 24 25 26 27 / LP-CD / 10 9 8 7 6 5 4 3 2 1

Every little **boy** and **girl** can be **afraid** about **something** at **some time.**

Being **afraid** means **you** have **fear.** Having **fear** can **be** a **good** thing...or a **bad** thing.

Fear is a **good thing** when it **warns you** about a **dangerous person**...or **place**...or **thing**...or **situation.**

For example, if **you** are **afraid** to **touch** a certain **animal,** then your **fear** might **be** a **good thing** because it may be **protecting you** from **danger.**

God allows us to be afraid of dangerous things so we will not get hurt.

Another **example** of **good fear** is if **you** are **afraid** to **cross** the **street** by **yourself**.

Being **afraid** to go **anyplace** where your **mom**...or **dad**...or **grandpa**...or **grandma**...or **someone** who takes **care** of **you**...tells you **not** to go is a **good fear**.

When **people** who **care** about **you** tell you **not** to **do** something, it is **because** they **love you** and want **you** to be **safe**.

It is always **good** to **obey** your **mom** and **dad**. It's **always** good to **obey God** too.

There is **bad fear** too. It is the **kind** of **fear** that makes you **scared** that something **bad** is **going** to **happen** to **you**...or to **someone**...or to **something** you **love**.

Jesus doesn't **want** you to have **bad fear**. **He wants** little **children** to **come** to **Him** when they are **afraid**. He **wants you** to **talk** to Him and **tell Him** what **scares** you, and **ask** Him to **take** your **fear away**. **Talking** to God is **praying**.

Jesus **listens** to the **prayers** of **children** as **carefully** as He **listens** to the **prayers** of **grown-ups**.

8

It is **possible** to be **afraid** of **something** that **doesn't** even **exist**.

For **example**, if you have a **bad dream** that makes you **afraid**, it is usually **because** of **something** you **saw**...or **heard about**...or **thought about** when **you** were **awake**.

A **dream** is what your mind **thinks about** when you are **sleeping**. Your **dream** is **not real**. You **are** having a **real dream**, but **what you** are **dreaming** is **not** really **happening**.

Have you **ever** had a **dream** that **seemed** very **real**, but when you **woke up**, you **realized** it wasn't **really happening**?

You can be **afraid** of **something** you think **might happen**. For example, **you** can be **afraid** that something **could** happen to **one** of your **pets**...or to **someone** you **love**...or to **one** of your **favorite** things. When you **feel afraid** that something **bad** might **happen**, tell **God**.

Lord, I am afraid that something might happen to my dog. Please keep him from being sick or hurt. Keep him from running away. If he does run away, help someone good to find him, and take care of him, and bring him back to me.

Some **children** are **afraid** of the **dark.** When they **can't see,** then they may **imagine things** that are **not there.**

If that ever **happens** to **you,** just **remember** that **God** is always **watching** over **you, even** in the **nighttime.** God **doesn't sleep.** He **doesn't need** to because **He** is **God. He** is **always awake.**

Talk to **God** every **night before** you **go** to **bed.**

Dear Lord, thank You
that You are always with me
and watching over me. I am glad
You can see everything...
even in the dark.

Sometimes boys and girls feel **afraid** at **night** that there could be **something scary** in their **closet**...or **under** the **bed**...or **behind** the **door**.

If **you** ever **feel afraid** about **that, ask** whoever is **taking care** of you to **turn on** the **light** and **show** you **your** closet...and **under** your **bed**...and **behind** the **door** so **you** can **see** that **nothing scary** is there.

> Dear Lord, thank You that You are always with me to protect me. Thank You that You care when I am afraid.

One day you may see **something** that **makes** you **afraid.** And that **scary thing** can **stay** in your **mind** so that you **remember** it **over** and **over.**

If that ever **happens** to you, **turn away** and **don't look** at **anything** that **scares** you. Ask **God** to help you **stop thinking** about the **scary thing** you saw.

Lord, I saw something that scared me. Please take that memory out of my mind so I won't think about it and be afraid anymore. Help me to think about things that make me happy. Help me think about things that make You happy too.

Loud sounds can **frighten** you—**especially** if they happen **suddenly,** and you **don't know** what they are.

Sometimes **even** when you **do** know **what** the **sound** is, it can **still scare** you. For example, some **children** are **afraid** of **loud thunder.**

If loud **thunder frightens** you, **see** if you **can go** to another **room** where it is **not** so **loud.** Tell **God** about any **noise** that is **scaring** you.

Lord, please help me to not be afraid when I hear thunder. Help me to remember that thunder is good because it brings rain and gives us water.

Have **you** ever been around **someone** who makes you **afraid?** You can be **afraid** of **people** who **aren't** very **nice.** Maybe they are **too rough**...or they are **too loud**...or they say **mean things** to other **people.** If that **happens** to you, tell your **mom** or **dad** how **afraid** you **are** of that **person.** Tell **other people** too. Tell **God how** that **person makes** you **feel.**

Lord, I am afraid of this person. Keep me away from him until You teach him how to have a kind and gentle heart.

Grown-ups can be afraid too. Even Jesus' disciples were sometimes afraid.

Once Jesus and His disciples were in a boat on a lake. That night a big storm came up. The disciples were so afraid that they woke Jesus and asked Him to help them.

Jesus **told** the **storm** to stop...and it **stopped**. The **disciples** were **amazed** that He could **do** that. They **forgot** that **God** was **with** them.

You need to **remember** that **God** is with **you** too.

Say, "**Thank** You, **Jesus**, that **You** are **always with** me, and every **time I pray,** You **hear** me."

Have **you** ever been **afraid** of getting **lost?** If that happens to you, remember that God **always sees** you.

God always **knows where** you **are.** You are **never alone** because **He** is always **with you.** That's why **you** can **never** be **lost** to **Him.**

If you **ever** do get **lost,** ask **God** to send **someone** to **find** you and **help** you **get** to **where** you need to **go.**

Lord, I thank You that You always see me. Keep me safe so I never get lost. But if I do get lost, help me to be found.

The **Bible** says **God's love** for **us** is so **strong** that it **takes away** our **fear**.

Did you **know** that **singing** a **song** to **God** can also **take away** your **fear?** That's **because** it is **one** of the **ways** we **show love** to God and say, **"Thank** You, **God**, for **loving me."**

It makes **God happy** to **hear** you **sing** a **song** to say you **love Him**. You can **make up** your own **melody**. Try **singing** this:

"**Thank** You, **Lord**, that You **love** me. I **love** You too. You are **always good** to me in **everything** You **do**."

Most of the **time** you will **not** be **afraid.** You will **laugh** and **play** and **run** and **be happy.**

You will have **people around** you who **love you** and **take** good **care** of **you.** They will **read books** to you...and **give** you **hugs**...and **kisses**...and **talk** to you about **everything.**

But **don't forget** to **talk** to **God** every day. He **always** wants to **hear** from **you.**

Thank You, God, for my happy life. Thank You for all my friends and family. Thank You that You love me so much.

When You Are Afraid, Say and Do These 7 Things

1. I remember that God is always with me, and I am never alone.

2. I pray to God and tell Him about what makes me afraid.

3. I tell other people who love me and take care of me about why I am afraid.

4. I ask someone from my family or friends to pray with me.

5. I thank God that His love takes away all my fear.

6. I remind God that I love Him.

7. I think about the things that make me happy, and I thank God for them.

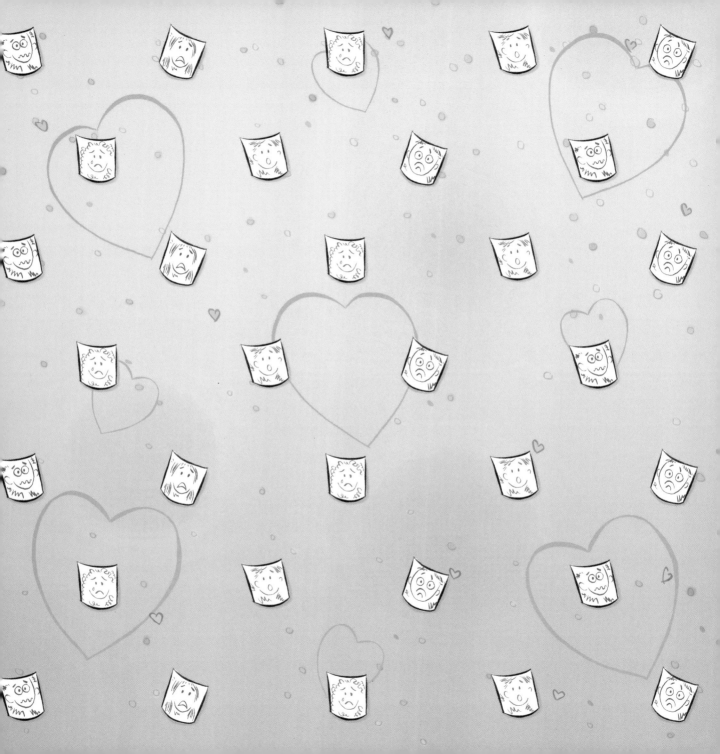